Latin Class trip to
Italy

BRUNO DOZZINI

GIOTTO

THE «LEGEND OF ST. FRANCIS» IN THE ASSISI BASILICA

EDITRICE MINERVA
1992

ENGLISH TRANSLATION by THE NEW SCHOOL – S. Maria degli Angeli

Photo – GERHARD RUF

© soc. coop. a.r.l.
EDITRICE MINERVA – ASSISI

INTRODUCTION

This publication does not claim to be scientific in nature. It originated as a guide for discriminating tourists, and not as a critical essay. Its contents are simply the result of individual research that may not be exhaustive but that was always nourished by my love for Francis of Assisi and for the works that Giotto did in his prime. I have intentionally neglected the debate over the attributions of the Legend of St. Francis: from Witte (1821) through Smart (1960), this issue has raised doubts as to Giotto's authorship of the cycle on account of stylistic and spatial divergences found between his works in Assisi and those he did in Padua.

Italian critics have always considered this doubt a groundless one, citing a lack of any substantial differences between these two cycles. One thing that is certain is the fact that Giotto was assisted by many apprentices, since Pope Boniface VIII had summoned him to Rome in 1300.

It has been said that Cimabue and Pietro Cavallini were among Giotto's teachers and that consequently, the Roman and Tuscan traditions were supposedly renewed and united triumphantly in his art. The famous anecdote about Cimabue's meeting with the poor young sheperd in the mountains along the Mugello Valley was first published by Lorenzo Ghiberti in 1455, but according to Berenson, if Giotto was indebted to anyone, it was not to Cimabue but to Cavallini. In fact, according to his first critic, Dante Alighieri, Giotto apparently even surpassed Cimabue. Around 1310, in Canto XI of Purgatorio in the Divine Comedy, Dante spoke through Oderisi of Gubbio, the great illuminator of manuscripts:

> In painting Cimabue thought indeed
> To hold the field; now Giotto has the cry
> So that the fame of the other few now heed.

But why is Giotto considered the greatest Italian Gothic painter?
Perhaps we can respond by saying that he is the one who made the most obvious break with Byzantine conventionality, drawing inspiration from a greater dramatic force or in other words, from a more animated representation of life. In Byzantine painting, the artist took pleasure in color effects, whereas in Giotto's paintings, everything is aimed toward sculptural emphasis. The figure, conceived here as a dominant element, does not pursue gracefulness but implies depth of feeling. Its stillness contributes to the expressive force of the image itself, giving it a majestic aspect. If, indeed, we see living beings that are proportionately larger than trees, mountains and objects, it is not so much the result of a « hierarchical scale » inherited from Byzantine art as it is an affirmation of the protagonists' control over the event they represent. In essence, the increase in volume augments the importance of what that volume represents. With Giotto, backgrounds are no longer full of allusions, nor are they made of solid gold. They appear instead as trees, mountains, skies, crowds and individuals, and include nudes that we can assert were the first ones to be seen in Italian painting. In Giotto's art, painting conquered complete freedom of inspiration and discovered the novelty of moving onward from allegory to story, an issue that had never been faced before in painting.

If we observe the figure of Francis portrayed in the Lower Church, Cimabue's Francis, he looks like the weak, emaciated, physical Francis, whereas with Giotto, he becomes Francis the giant, the hero of the story who is brought back to the source of biblical spirituality.

The art of painting, an art that had been dead for centuries, had its renaissance in Giotto — and this has been stated by a number of people including Boccaccio, Villani and Sacchetti. He transformed Byzantine iconic immobility into monumental grandeur, and tragedy into drama.

Giotto contrasts his art, an art that says everything human and divine, against art that does not speak because it is ineffable.

These frescoes must be interpreted in a religious, artistic and social vein. (They should be viewed starting on the left-hand side when facing away from the main altar).

They must been seen from a religious perspective, first of all because the paintings are in a holy place, secondly because they portray the life of a saint and finally, because Giotto's art is equivalent to veneration.

In fact, to a man and artist of the Middle Ages, reality was first and foremost a religious reality.

For example, one could say that the high point of medieval poetry was *The Canticle of the Creatures*, a three-dimensional hymn revolving around God, man and nature in an essentially joint relationship that is never broken and that will never be broken. Thus, the religious aspect cannot be extirpated from this triad and consequently, it is always a unitary relationship. Giotto's painting is indeed unitary because it is religious and it is religious because it is unitary. It is not enough just to acknowledge that the artist has aesthetic unity. In fact, it would be a grave error to classify him simply as an innovator of form and technique. Technical and structural innovations cannot exist if there is no pre-existing action or determination made of flesh and of ideas. This is the summa that has been handed down to us by the Middle Ages through St. Thomas Aquinas in philosophy, through Dante in poetry, and through Giotto in painting.

The visitor who has grasped this discussion will be in a position to reconstruct all of Francis' spiritual greatness and Giotto's artistic greatness. Thus the artistic interpretation cannot ignore the religious interpretation: the two complement each other.

As to the social interpretation, we can say that it is interesting in terms of that multiplicity from which no true art can escape. It is a multiplicity, however, that can also be cloaked in bitterness toward genius or in cultural presumptions that have little or nothing in common with history. Read the commentaries on frescoes 5, 6 and 15 in order to gain some insight as to the highly debatable interpretations that can be made by captious positivistic critics who willingly ignore the anagogical meaning of the paintings, that being the meaning that teaches us how we should conform our lives to the will of God.

Bear in mind that the abbreviations listed on the lower right-hand side at the beginning of the commentary on each fresco refer to the « Franciscan Sources » (*St. Francis of Assisi, Writings and Early Biographies: English Omnibus of Sources for the Life of St. Francis*) that recount the various episodes. See page 64 for an explanation of these abbreviations.

I feel obliged to say that I have omitted any analysis of the relationships existing among all the paintings on the walls of the nave, even though such an analysis is extremely interesting from an eschatological point of view. Here I am referring to the Old and New Testament cycles that are divided into two bands above Giotto's cycle. I do feel, however, that it would be useful to advise the reader to bear in mind that the 28 frescoes are not a true biography of Francis (for example, the birth of the saint as well as many other aspects of his life are missing) but a demonstration and an exhortation as to how man must conform to God's will so he can become what the Gospel calls « the New Man. » Thus, the link connecting the three cycles of paintings emerges automatically: the Adamite period (Old Testament – Adam as the First Man); the Christological period (New Testament - Christ as a second Adam); the Franciscan Period (Giotto's cycle – Francis as the « New Man » who conformed himself to Christ). Without invoking any Joachimist ancestors, which are evident in any case, we can affirm that a tight bond, more theological than historical in nature, connects the cycles, offering a concise indication of the main path to human salvation. Consequently, the figure of Francis becomes part of the Deesis represented by John the Baptist (personification of the Old Testament) and Mary (personification of the New Testament) who intercede with Christ, the universal Judge, on man's behalf. With Francis, the New Man born of Christ, the Deesis is enriched even further, and the emphasis is placed on the on-going work of bearing the message of the Old and New Testaments (see the four medallions in the central vault of the nave of the Upper Church, attributed to Jacopo Torriti, as well as other examples such as Pietro Lorenzetti's « Madonna of the Sunsets » in the left transept of the Lower Church, or the triptych, also by Lorenzetti, in the chapel of St. John the Baptist). One detail that cannot be deemed insignificant also lies in the fact that, from the viewer's standpoint, Francis is always shown turned toward the right, with the exception of panels 5 and 6, in which he is obeying the voice of God. In these two instances, Francis is in greater need of drawing from God the strength that his physical body cannot offer him.

Remember that 26 of the 28 frescoes are 2.70 x 2.30 meters in size, each fresco thus covering an area of over six square meters. The other two frescoes, located on either side of the entrance, are smaller, although not by much. In fact, they are 2.70 x 2.00 meters in size. The total painted surface thus equals 172 square meters. Each fresco has a titulus running beneath it in a narrow light-blue band.

The titles are written in Latin and we have listed these captions in both Latin and English on the pages illustrating each painting. Most of the frescoes were restored around 1970 and were cleaned even more recently of all the dust raised by the incessant shuffling of the great numbers of pilgrims, tourists, researchers and simple onlookers from all over the world. Unfortunately, the numerous dry touch-ups that Giotto was accustomed to doing on the paintings have since disappeared.

Therefore, through Giotto's magnificent and innovative work, we can gain an illustration of a good part of the life of St. Francis, a man like others, a man with others, a man for others, yet a man so different from the rest that, as stated by Joseph Lortz, one of the greatest German historians, « Francis is the most authentic image to be found in universal sainthood. »

CUM VIR SIMPLEX DE ASSISIO STERNIT VESTES BEATO FRANCISCO FU-
DITQUE HONORES IPSI EUNTI, SUPER HOC, CREDITUR, ERUDITUS A DEO, AS-
SERENS OMNI FRANCISCUM REVERENTIA DIGNUM, QUIA ESSET IN PROXIMO
MAGNA FACTURUS, ET IDEO AB OMNIBUS HONORANDUS.

When a citizen of the town of Assisi, a very simple man, spread his cloak down before
Blessed Francis; in addition to this, it is believed that upon meeting him, a very learned
person poured forth his praise, saying that Francis deserved everyone's respect because
soon he would do great things; thus he should be honored by all.

[LM I, 1]

1 - Homage of a Simple Man

This painting depicts the episode of a poor man who, almost as a prediction of Francis' glorious future, lays his cloak down beneath the saint's feet. The man did this every time he happened to meet him. It seems that his name was Gino della Fagiola, although he could also have been a man of culture, as stated in the titulus as well. If we want to interpret this episode from a symbolic viewpoint as well, we could say that it shows a meeting with a madman who, thanks precisely to lunacy's mysterious power to foretell the future, sees a very great destiny for the other man. In this scene, Francis is less than 24 years old, which is how old he was in 1206 when the Crucifix spoke to him in the rustic oratory at San Damiano. Francis is still wearing rich clothing and shoes and is accompanied by his friends, members of Assisi's rich bourgeoisie. This is an episode that shows Francis who is not a saint yet, although Giotto has placed a halo over his head. It has been asserted that this panel was painted last due to the work being done to construct the rood-screen on that part of the wall. The colors in this painting are somewhat faded, especially at the roof-top terraces on the right and on the saint's tunic. These ruined areas of color occur frequently in the panels of this cycle because Giotto was accustomed to doing some of his finishing touches with tempera on dry plaster and since these touch-ups were obviously more subject to deterioration, they chipped off over the centuries. Observe the saint's halo, which is done in relief and is particularly elaborate. It would seem that the halo, together with the saint's head, may have required a full day of work. Also interesting are some of the details that, by being removed from historical reality, constitute a sort of "artistic license" that occurred quite frequently with Giotto. For example, the Temple of Minerva, a classical work of the Augustan age, is depicted instead as an Arnolfo-style Gothic temple. Giotto painted it with five columns, whereas the temple actually has six. The Tower of the People did not exist during Francis' time because its construction began in 1275 and ended in 1305. At the time of Francis' death (1226), the Palace of the Captain of the People had been under construction for just a few years (it was started in 1212) and it was finished in 1282, so that he could not have seen its completion. Note the crenelation on these two palaces: the original crenelation on the Tower of the People was Ghibelline, whereas the modern crenelation (1926) on the Palace of the Captain of the People is Guelph. Although the pronaos of the temple has remained unchanged since the Augustan age of ancient Rome, in 1539 the cell was transformed into a Christian church called Santa Maria sopra Minerva and then it was reconstructed in a Baroque style by Giacomo Giorgetti in 1634. The church was later dedicated to St. Philip Neri during the eighteenth century.

CUM BEATUS FRANCISCUS OBVIUM HABUIT MILITEM QUEMDAM GENERO-SUM SED PAUPEREM ET MALE VESTITUM, CUIUS PAUPERIEM PIO MISERATUS AFFECTU, ILLUM PROTINUS, SE EXUTO, VESTIVIT.

When Blessed Francis met a knight who was of noble birth but very poor and poorly clad. Francis felt sorry for his miserable state and immediately took off his mantle to clothe the poor man.

[LM I, 2; 2 Cel. 5]

2 - Francis gives his cloak to the poor fallen knight

Going in chronological order, this was the first episode that Giotto painted. The figures here already set the formula of spatial rhythm typical of Giotto, as well as the elements characteristic of his artistic language. Giotto uses the lines of the mountains to draw the diagonals of the square, placing the saint's head at their point of intersection. The viewer's eye is immediately attracted to this ideal center, and in fact, it becomes precisely the central point irradiating a movement that expands to fill the entire space. Furthermore, the pathos here does not stem from excited gestures but is the result of the moral order of human behavior. In this panel, the figures do not yet have that three-dimensional aspect that would later appear in Giotto's work. The space is constructed as an inclined and rocky plane on which the figures rest. All the viewer needs to do to realize this is to look at the position of Francis' feet, which seem to be turned upward, just as in the old Byzantine mosaics. The azure triangle of the sky, inlaid between the brown triangles of the mountains, suggests esoteric significance. The folds of the cloak are made even more evident by the lighter and darker areas imparted by the heightening technique typical of previous artistic styles. Some critics refuse to believe that Giotto anticipated the Renaissance, since the poetics of man as « the center of the universe » are removed from or even opposed to Giotto's poetics, which instead are directed towards the totality of creation, which obviously includes God, man, animals and things. Giotto creates typologies, not individuals. He expresses collective sentiments, as was done moreover throughout the Middle Ages. Giotto's art is classical because it has an overall conception of reality, which is expressed through the equilibrium of the closed masses and which, as in Francis' message itself, fulfills all things throughout the universe. From a symbolic viewpoint, the fresco is divided into two sections, almost as if to show the class division into maiores and minores and the separation between secular and religious life. In fact, shown on the left is the city of Assisi as seen from Porta Nuova and on the right is the Abbey of San Benedetto, which is on the mountainside. So here we have city and country, the middle class and the farmers, Francis − representative of Assisi's rich bourgeoisie − and the noble fallen knight. The two men, who are practically united by the cloak, are already an expression of the human solidarity proclaimed by Francis in the name of social and ecclesiastical reform. Observe the expression of fervent charity that makes the saint seem seraphic: charity is the first step foreshadowing his imitation of Christ. Some scholars have also compared this fresco to Simone Martini's painting in the Lower Church illustrating St. Martin who shares his cloak with a poor man. Such a comparison is very important yet subtly different, even though at first glance, these two acts of charity could appear to be analogous. Nevertheless, they are not comparable because they differ in meaning. St. Martin's act is a pure and simple act of charity towards a poor man, whereas the action of St. Francis, who instead of sharing his mantle gives it away completely, is an act that, while being an act of love, also foretells his determination to draw the two social classes together. The recipient is not a poor man but a fallen nobleman and in fact, during the thirteenth century, the nobility yielded to the rising middle class in both position and importance. In this painting, as in the one before it, areas of deterioration can be seen on the tunics of both the saint as well as the knight. This deterioration is due to Giotto's use of tempera to touch up his works.

CUM BEATUS FRANCISCUS NOCTE SEQUENTI SE SOPORI DEDISSET, PALA-
TIUM SPECIOSUM ET MAGNUM CUM MILITARIBUS ARMIS CRUCIS CHRISTI SI-
GNACULO INSIGNITIS VIDIT, ET CUM QUAERERET CUIUS ESSENT, ILLA OM-
NIA SUA FORE MILITUMQUE SUORUM SUPERNA FUIT ASSERTIONE RESPON-
SUM.

How the next night, as Blessed Francis lay in a deep sleep, he saw in a dream a magnificent palace full of armor bearing Christ's cross, and when he asked to whom all this belonged, he was told from heaven that it was all for him and his followers.

[LM I, 3; 2 Cel. 6]

3 - Vision of the palace

In 1205, in an attempt to comply with the wishes of his father, Pietro di Bernardone, who wanted him to become a merchant or better yet a knight, Francis, Assisi's « king of parties », departed from Assisi to join Walter III of Brienne (1165-1205), known as « Count Gentile ». With the approval of Innocent III, Walter of Brienne was preparing to leave on an armed expedition against the kingdom of Sicily. At the end of this expedition, he died in Sarno, in the southern Italian region of Campania. After the first day's journey southward, the platoon Walter had recruited in Assisi stopped to rest among the age-old oaks of Monteluco, near Spoleto. Here, Francis fell ill and dreamed of Christ, who showed him a large and splendid palace with coats of arms and banners adorned with His cross. When Francis asked to whom they belonged, a celestial voice answered in a friendly tone that they were all for him and for his knights. Then the voice added, « Francis, who can do more for you, a Lord or his servant, a rich man or a poor man? » And since Francis replied that surely a Lord or a rich man could do more, the voice continued, « Then why are you abandoning the Lord to devote yourself to a servant? Why are you choosing a beggar instead of God, who is infinitely rich? » So Francis replied, « Lord, what will you have me do? » « Go back to your own town. The vision that you saw foretold a spiritual achievement which will be accomplished in you by God's will, not man's. » The exhortation to « go back to your own town » is reminiscent of the one addressed to Saul: « Get up and go into the city, where you will be told what to do » (Acts 9,6) and it also recalls the Lord's words to Jacob: « Go back to the land of your birth, and I will be good to you » (Gen 32,10). Francis then understood that he was to go on a different crusade, the crusade of the spirit, and after he returned to Assisi, he made a pilgrimage to Rome. The scene is divided into two areas: in the foreground on the left is the room in which Francis is lying ill. Standing next to him is Christ, who is pointing to a symbolic palace on the right that is placed on a slightly retreating plane. This alludes to the Francis' future army. The vision of the palace with the crossed coats of arms and banners could also symbolize Francis' profound indecision over whether to follow the path of worldly glory (the coats of arms) or the path of spiritual adventure (the banner with the cross). There are deteriorated areas in the lower part of the fresco and on the head of Christ. Christ's mantle was originally illuminated with gold, but this has now disappeared. The three frescoes we have examined so far develop a unitary concept that is articulated in three consecutive steps: prediction, generosity, reward.

*CUM BEATUS FRANCISCUS ORARET ANTE IMAGINEM CRUCIFIXI, VOX DILAP-
SA EST DE CRUCE TER DICENS: FRANCISCE, VADE REPARA DOMUM MEAM:
QUAE TOTA DESTRUITUR: PER HOC ROMANAM SIGNIFICANS ECCLESIAM.*

As Blessed Francis was praying before a painted image of the Crucified, he heard a voice
coming from the cross and telling him three times, « Francis, go and repair my house. You
see it is all falling down, » and this alluded to the Church of Rome.

[LM II, 1; 2 Cel. 10]

4 - The Miracle of the Crucifix

As we said in our remarks about Francis' dream at Monteluco of Spoleto, Francis had gone to Rome on a pilgrimage. In 1206, following his return to Assisi, he went into the countryside to meditate one day and on impulse, he went into the ruined little chapel of San Damiano. Here, the image on a painted Crucifix said to him three times, « Francis, go and repair my house, which, as you can see, is falling completely to ruin ». Since he did not understand the significance of this command, Francis thought he was to repair the dilapidated chapel. He improvised as a mason and repaired three churches (San Damiano, Santa Maria di Giosafat, or the Porziuncola, and San Pietro della Spina), begging throughout the city of Assisi for the bricks he needed. It is assumed that he had already learned how to use a trowel and mortar at the age of sixteen (1198), when he participated with the people of Assisi who had united to rebel against Duke Conrad of Lützen. At that time, he aided in the destruction of the fortress of Barbarossa (built in 1174) and in the incredibly fast construction of Assisi's city walls, whose size alone can attest to the energy the entire population of the town had exerted to build them. As we know, however, two more years were to pass after the Crucifix told Francis what to do before he understood that the church he was to repair, the one that was in ruins, was the church of the spirit, the church that, starting with its terrestrial hierarchies, must live within each of us. And he had this new revelation on February 24th, 1208 (according to other scholars, it took place on October 18th, 1209) in the little church of the Porziuncola, which he was still in the process of restoring. This revelation came to him through a Gospel passage about the *missio apostolorum*, which Francis asked the priest to explain further. Nevertheless, it immediately became apparent to him that this was the path to follow. This was the first time he truly took the habit. In fact, it was in this manner that a profound vocation to the moral reformation of the Church began to ferment within him. Francis is kneeling inside the small dilapidated chapel that symbolically represents the entire church, buffeted by the winds of heresy, hypocrisy, immorality and arrogance. Nevertheless, the faith of the saint seems to be unshakeable and although he is surrounded by nothing by ruins, he is engrossed in prayer. In fact, he is still sheltered in the safest part of the building, whereas the Crucifix itself is completed exposed to the winds of time. The Crucifix that speaks to Francis is a twelfth-century Byzantine image painted on wood, done by an anonymous artist. The mourners, shown in full figure, are next to Jesus, who is portrayed as the living and triumphant Christ (*Christus Triumphans*). From Francis' time on, the image of Christus Patiens would prevail. Today, the original of this Crucifix can be seen in the Basilica of Santa Chiara, whereas the one on the altar at San Damiano is a twentieth-century copy done by Brother Leone Bracaloni. A curious detail that deserves mention, although it is an aspect that can also be found in Giotto's other works, is his abundant use of artistic license. With Giotto's brush stokes, in fact, the poor rustic oratory of San Damiano becomes a great church with Romanesque windows and it is even sustained by columns. The foreshortened architecture should also be noted: many critics have often thought this to anticipate Giotto's more mature spatial language. The painting reveals extensive damage on the left-hand side and art historian Salvini reports that a small amount of work was done by Giotto's school.

CUM RESTITUIT PATRI OMNIA, ET, VESTIMENTIS DEPOSITIS, RENUNTIAVIT BONIS PATERNIS ET MUTABILIBUS, DICENS AD PATREM: AMODO SECURE DICERE POSSUM « PATER NOSTER QUI ES IN COELIS » CUM REPUDIAVERIT ME PETRUS BERNARDONIS.

When he gave everything back to his father. Having taken off his clothes, he renounced all his claims to fleeting worldly goods, saying to his father, « From now on I can freely say « Our Father who art in heaven,' since Pietro di Bernardone has disowned me. »

[LM II, 14; 1 Cel. 14; 2 Cel. 14; Three Comp. VI, 20]

16

5 - Renunciation of worldly goods

In 1207, standing before Bishop Guido and a great crowd that had gathered at the bishop's palace in Assisi, the saint gave every object and every item of clothing back to his father, Pietro di Bernardone. He renounced all his possessions to the point that he was left stark naked and the bishop was forced to cover him with his mantle. This image, together with the one depicted on the left wall of the Lower Church, is probably one of the first "rules" in Italian painting. The scene took place in public because Pietro di Bernardone hoped to convince Francis to change his strange behavior once he was face-to-face with the authority of the church, as represented by Guido. Instead, Francis reasserted his determination to restore everything by renouncing his father's property. He said to his father, « From now on I can say without reserve Our Father who art in heaven, since Pietro di Bernardone has disowned me. » The painting shows us the moment in which Francis invokes the Eternal, who may have been depicted in the upper left, where instead there is only a benedictory white hand. However, the fact that this upper area is very deteriorated could lend support to the theory that the body of the Eternal was also portrayed there at one time. Francis' father is held back by one of his attendants (perhaps his other son, Angelo) because otherwise, he would hurl himself against his degenerate son. In the meantime, two children have already gathered some stones and are ready to fling them at Francis since they think he is mad. We know that after this outstanding event, Francis went to Gubbio to stay with the family of Federico Spadalonga, who later donated his house so a church could be built in Francis' honor: this church still exists in Gubbio. The saint received his first coarse homespun tunic from his friend, Jacobello Spadalonga. This type of tunic later became the Franciscan habit as we know it today, with the triple-knotted cord down the side. The benedictory hand of the Eternal is on the same perpendicular as Pietro di Bernardone's clenched fist, or in any case, it is over his head: just as heaven blesses, the world condemns and tries to solve problems with violence. Above the empty din of the crowd, Francis, having divested himself of the insignias of Assisi's middle class, announces his noble and shining ideal of complete poverty, which must also coincide with the complete deprivation of self. Some have also taken Guido's mantle to signify Francis' profession and taking of the habit under ecclesiastical authority, or at the very least, under the Church's protection. On one side of the scene are the furious relatives and the mindless crowds, and on the other side is the saint, together with the bishops and priests. The architectural structures hanging over these two groups emphasize their contrasting emotions, since on the left are the houses of the rich middle classes, whereas on the right there is a group of shrine-like buildings which, while not in the form of a church, are clearly sacred in nature. The expressive unity of the figures and of the architectural structures that move toward the ideal center of the painting is evident. The center is empty but it does not represent an insurmountable lack of communication, since Francis' arms are stretched out in hope. The group on the left is more numerous because in this world, it is the majority that remains silent, indifferent and hostile before the truth that Francis teaches by freeing himself of all superfluous things in order to gain man's salvation.

QUOMODO PAPA VIDEBAT LATERANENSEM BASILICAM FORE PROXIMAM IAM RUINAE, QUAM QUIDAM PAUPERCULUS, SCILICET BEATUS FRANCISCUS, PROPRIO DORSO SUBMISSO, NE CADERET, SUBSTENTABAT.

How the Pope saw in a dream that the Lateran Basilica was about to fall to ruin when a miserable little poor man, that is, Blessed Francis, propped it up by putting his own back under it lest it fall.

[LM III, 10; 2 Cel. 16, 17]

6 - Dream of Innocent III

Brother Giuliano da Spira closely identified the fundamental values of Minorite ecumenism and apostolicity with the moral figure of St. Francis. Here we see Francis holding up the Lateran Basilica, a cathedral in Rome that is traditionally the Pope's See, while Innocent III dreams of a friar who is taller and stouter than the very columns, almost like a second Samson, who sustains the temple with his powerful shoulder to keep it from collapsing. This fresco, painted entirely by Giotto himself, should be viewed not only in a religious context but in a social one as well. However, any social interpretation should be done with extreme care to avoid allowing it degenerate into a political interpretation. In fact, this is precisely what happened when certain positivistic critics tried to read into the Assisi series, and into Giotto's cycle in particular, a sign of the political power held by Boniface VIII and the Roman Curia. According to these exegetes, Francis was supposedly deprived of his personal strength and transformed into a hero of the Roman primate. Their argument was simple: as the Pope, unwarlike and almost oblivious of his great task, slept peacefully beneath rich blankets, Francis took upon himself the entire weight of the church, essentially acting as an instrument to uphold the temporal power of the papacy. However, the theory that the *longa manus*, or the long hand of the Roman Curia had intruded upon the series and upon the iconographic plans in Assisi cannot be sustained. While it is true that Gregory IX stimulated the construction of the sanctuary, asking all of Christianity to contribute, other popes (Nicholas III and Nicholas IV), cardinals (Orsini, Montefiore, Albornoz) and bishops (Pontano) were also responsible for commissioning the church, not to make the sanctuary into an *instrumentum regni* but out of devotion to the saint whose protection they wanted. One should also bear in mind that what is shown in this fresco is the fulfillment of what the crucifix at San Damiano had ordered Francis to do, and not the execution of an order coming from the ecclesiastical hierarchy. It is interesting to consider and to compare Cimabue's Francis with Giotto's. Cimabue's work (and I am referring here to the right transept of the Lower Church) shows us the human, almost fragile and trembling portrait of Francis that he had gleaned from Tommaso of Celano's *First Life*. In the Franciscan cycle of the Upper Church, on the other hand, Giotto offers us a moral portrait of the religious reformer who addressed his sublime teachings to all creatures through his example rather than his words. From this panel on, Francis is shown wearing a habit rather than the light-blue tunic. The habit is better preserved in these frescoes because it was all done using the "a fresco" or wet-plaster technique, whereas with the light-blue tunic, lapis-lazuli was brushed on "a secco", or on dry plaster. Several researchers have noted that the spatial arrangement of the right-hand side of the painting has been weakened by the disappearance of a chest, which had been painted on dry plaster, that was positioned between the Pope and the two seated characters. St. Francis is portrayed here as being as smooth-faced as Apollo: he is the incarnation of eternal youth and absolute perfection.

CUM PAPA APPROBAVIT REGULAM ET DEDIT DE POENITENTIA PRAEDICAN-
DA MANDATUM, ET FRATRIBUS, QUI SANCTUM FUERANT COMITATI, FECIT CO-
RONAS FIERI, UT VERBUM DEI PRAEDICARENT.

When the Pope approved the rule and gave the friars who had joined the saint a mission
to preach repentance, conferring the clerical tonsure so they could preach the word of God.

[LM III, 10; I Cel. 33]

7 - Confirmation of the rule

When Innocent III found himself face-to-face with Francis, who had gone to Rome in 1209 to ask the pope to approve the rule (or rather, the « way of life ») he had drawn up together with his original twelve companions in the hovel at Rivotorto, he recognized in Francis the friar who had sustained the tottering Lateran Basilica in his dream. As a result, he authorized him to preach the Gospel. This was not a true confirmation of the Minorite rule but merely oral permission to preach repentance. In view of the revolutionary nature of the Franciscan message, one may well ask how this aspect could be consistent with Francis' desire always to obtain the consent of the highest ecclesiastical institutions. The answer is not an easy one. Francis' revolution attempts to work from within. In other words, it is a revolution that cannot ignore the Church. Francis sensed that without the Church's approval, his movement would be destroyed. He was certain that only within the Church could he carry out his desire to follow Christ. In fact, how could he have left the Church after the command handed down to him by the Crucifix at San Damiano, which had ordered him to repair that very church? Thus, it was not servile acquiescence or fear of responsibility that induced Francis to follow the humiliating path separating him from the throne of the powerful. Francis told the Pontiff a parable about a rich monarch who had had three children by a poor but very beautiful woman who lived in the desert because people spurned her. The children resembled the king, so they were raised in his royal palace and were accorded all honor. The meaning of this parable, which had been suggested to Francis by the Holy Spirit, is that those who imitate the king (Jesus Christ) and who were begotten in his likeness by a poor yet beautiful mother (Poverty) will have everything they need bestowed upon them. The Pope became convinced that, as in the parable, Francis would truly support the Church of Christ with his works and his doctrine, and not just in a dream. Then the Pope conferred small tonsures on all the lay brothers who had accompanied Francis so that, by law, they could freely teach the Gospel. The lay brothers portrayed by Giotto already have tonsures. This panel is very interesting for a number of reasons, first of all because of the two doors implying great esoteric significance and secondly because of the amazement expressed by the bishops of the official Church. Furthermore, the characters are portrayed in profile, whereas in art before Giotto's time, they were always portrayed frontally. Finally, the architectural background is shown in perspective. As we have already mentioned several times, Giotto overturned this tradition. There is yet another consideration to be made concerning the two groups of characters facing each other. The group on the right is the image of the temporal Church, whereas the group on the left represents the spiritual Church. And just as the Pope, patriarch of all Christians, is shown blessing Francis, the patriarch Isaac is also blessing Jacob in the Old Testament fresco above. Both Francis and Jacob are indeed the founding fathers of two new generations.

CUM BEATUS FRANCISCUS ORARET IN QUODAM TUGURIO ET CUM SUI FRATRES ESSENT IN ALIO TUGURIO EXTRA CIVITATEM, QUIBUSDAM QUIESCENTIBUS ET QUIBUSDAM PERSEVERANTIBUS IN ORANDO, ET ILLE CORPORALITER ABSENTARETUR A FILIIS ECCE ISTI VIDERUNT PAULLO POST BEATUM FRANCISCUM IN CURRU IGNEO ET PERLUCIDO, PER DOMUM, FERE MEDIA NOCTIS HORA, VOLITARE, DUM MAGNA LUCE TUGURIUM RESPLENDUIT, UNDE OBSTUPEFACTI SUNT VIGILANTES, EXCITATI ET EXTERRITI DORMIENTES.

While Blessed Francis was praying in a hut and his brothers were in another hut outside the city, so that in person he was separated from the friars. And behold, about midnight when some of the brothers were resting and some were praying they saw Blessed Francis on a fiery chariot of extraordinary brilliance and the entire countrside was illuminated. Those who were awake were dumbfounded, while the others woke up terrified.   [LM IV, 4; 1 Cel. 47]

8 - Vision of the flaming chariot

In Rivotorto, a hamlet on the outskirts of Santa Maria degli Angeli named after a brook that winds its way through it, the brothers saw their father, Francis, being carried off into heaven at around midnight by a chariot of fire, just like the prophet Elijah. However, Francis was not with them because he had gone to Assisi. The next day, a Sunday, he was to preach at the cathedral as he usually did. When he returned, he began to penetrate the secrets of each friar's conscience and he also made many predictions about the future development of the Order. The meaning of this episode is that the friars were to follow Francis' leadership, just as the Israelites had followed the guidance of Elijah. Elijah was a biblical prophet who left no written records but who had a role of great importance in Israel's religious history. He was the only one, after Enoch, who was said to have been carried off into heaven and according to Jewish tradition, the Hebrews still await his return. Incidentally, we should remember that several Jews thought that Jesus was a second Elijah. Others felt that Jesus' last cry on the Cross (« Eloi, Eloi, lama sabachtani ») was an invocation to Elijah. The architecture of the primitive Franciscan « hovel » is concisely represented. Today, this hovel is preserved inside the Church of Santa Maria di Rivotorto, which was built in 1854 over foundations dating to the late sixteenth century. On the Gothic-style façade, there is a mosaic depicting Elijah in the flaming chariot and Emperor Otto IV, who passed through Rivotorto in 1209 on his way to Rome to be crowned by Innocent III. Note the amazed yet composed and dignified looks of the friars. St. Bonaventure said that by virtue of their perfect understanding, the friars were accustomed to seeing their inner thoughts reflected in each other's eyes. The cultured and classically idealized origin of the chariot, inspired by ancient decorative art, has been pointed out in this work by Giotto. It is difficult to see the saint's face because part of this fresco has faded.

CUM UNI FRATRI VISIO COELITUS OSTENSA MONSTRAVIT MULTAS IN COELO SEDES ET UNAM PRAE CETERIS DIGNIOREM OMNI GLORIA REFULGENTEM, ET AUDIVIT VOCEM DICENTEM SIBI: SEDES ISTA UNIUS DE RUENTIBUS ANGELIS FUIT, ET NUNC HUMILI SERVATUR FRANCISCO.

A heavenly vision that appeared to a little friar showed him many thrones in heaven, but one of these was more exalted and glorious than all the others. He heard a voice saying to him, « This throne belonged to one of the fallen angels, but now it is reserved for humble Francis. »

[LM VI, 9; 2 Cel. 122, 123; Mirror 60; Leg. Per. 23]

9 - Vision of the thrones

In the ancient church of San Pietro in Bovara (Trevi), Brother Leone, « the little lamb of God » as Francis called him, saw an angel who showed him the throne reserved for Francis in heaven, the throne that had once belonged to Lucifer. We should recall that, according to the ambiguous interpretive translation of the Vulgata, Lucifer is considered the leader of the demons who fell from heaven when they rebelled against God. Here, Francis and Lucifer have been placed side by side for the purpose of illustrating the saint's sublime humility through this contrast. The « father of the lesser brothers, » or Friars Minor, who was to occupy the throne once held by the « father of the proud, » poses a life example to be admired and, if possible, imitated. In this difficult to interpret fresco, Francis, after having been praised through his comparison to Old Testament figures such as Adam, Moses, Samson, Elias, Enoch, Joseph and so on, is praised exceptionally through a negative figure such as Lucifer. In Canto XI of Paradise, Dante himself called Assisi « the Orient » and Francis « the sun, » thus also lending support to the apocalyptic theory of the angel of the sixth seal (Rev 6, 12-17). This painting shows us the deep devotion felt already by the masses toward the prophetic figure of Francis, who instead considered himself the greatest of sinners. Some scholars have instead attributed Brother Leo's vision to Brother Pacifico (born Guglielmo Davini), a troubador who is traditionally said to have been crowned at the Capitol. The crowds had nicknamed him « the King of Verse » because of his fresh poetical vein. After he became a Friar Minor, he received the gift of vision and was named "Pacificus" by Francis himself because he had abandoned the roar of the crowds to attain the peace of God. Observe the lamp in front of the Crucifix. It can be raised or lowered at will by using the rope. Also note the strange shape of the central throne, which has four seats separated by low backs, forming an « X. » In effect, the throne can be reached from all from sides. Perhaps its meaning harks back to the very noble message contained in the last part of the Sacrum Commercium. Or perhaps it implies instead that Lucifer can enter the very heart of mankind from all sides.

CUM BEATUS FRANCISCUS VIDIT SUPRA CIVITATEM ARETII DAEMONES EXUL-TANTES ET AIT SOCIO: VADE, ET IN VIRTUTE DEI DAEMONES EXPELLE, SICUT IN DOMINO IPSO TIBI PRAESCRIPTUM EST, CLAMANS IN PORTA. UT AUTEM IL-LE OBOEDIENS CLAMAVIT, DAEMONES AUFUGERUNT, ET PAX ILLICO FACTA EST.

When Blessed Francis saw the devils rejoicing over the city of Arezzo, he spoke to one of his brothers, saying, « Go, and in the name of almighty God, send away the devils, as the Lord himself has ordered you to do. » Obeying, as soon as he began to cry aloud at the town gate, the demons fled and the city was immediately restored to peace.

[LM VI, 9; 2 Cel. 108]

10 - Exorcism of the demons from Arezzo

Following Francis' orders, Brother Silvestro exorcised the city of Arezzo, liberating her from the demons. The saint had sent ahead his companion, a man of dove-like simplicity, saying to him, « Go up to the town gate and in the name of almighty God, command the devils in virtue of obedience to go away immediately. » Being the genuinely obedient man that he was, Brother Silvestro hurried off to carry out the Father's orders and after he had prayed to the Lord, he began to cry aloud before the town gate, « In the name of almighty God and by the command of his servant Francis, away with you all you devils! » In this fresco, as in others we have seen, there is an aesthetic division into two separate sections. Portrayed on the left are the Gothic Duomo of Arezzo and Francis, who is praying, and shown on the right are the city inside the walls and the devils, who are fleeing from the houses through the chimneys. Obviously, the demons are none other than man's human and political passions − excessive power, corruption and factional hatred. It is interesting to note that the lacerating divisions between the social classes are also evident in the landscape, in which the main gate, used by the *maiores*, poses a sharp contrast to the narrower side gate, from which a farmer is leaving with his donkey. We cannot talk about true parties yet, since the Guelphs and the Ghibellines did not become parties until 1228. While he did influence the Italian society of his day, Francis was not an intentionally political figure. He saw evil in men only because they had drawn away from the Gospel.

CUM BEATUS FRANCISCUS OB CHRISTI FIDEM VOLUIT INTRARE IGNEM MA-
GNUM CUM SACERDOTIBUS SOLDANI BABILONIAE, SED NULLUS EORUM VO-
LUIT INTRARE CUM EO, SED STATIM DE SUIS CONSPECTIBUS AUFUGERUNT.

When Blessed Francis, because of the faith of Christ, wanted to go into a great fire together with the priests of the Sultan of Babylonia, but none of them were willing to enter
with him. Rather they fled quickly from the presence of the onlookers.

[LM IX, 8; 1 Cel. 57; LF 24]

11 - Trial by fire

This panel, most of which was not painted by Giotto himself, portrays Francis, « the herald of the great King, » as he proposes a trial by fire to the Sultan of Egypt, Melek-el-Kamel. The trial by fire was part of the so-called "ordeal", the results of which were supposed to be a direct response from God. The ordeal was used among many so-called primitive peoples and is also referred to in the Old Testament. It was unknown to the Romans but was popular among the Germanic peoples. The Church permitted the ordeal to be practiced during the early Middle Ages, but it then definitively condemned it during the Provincial Council of Valladolid (Spain) in 1322. In 1219, Francis embarked in Ancona for Acre and Damietta, the last Christian stronghold in the Holy Land, and he joined the crusaders between the fifth and sixth Crusades. He witnessed the siege and then the fall of Damietta and was horrified by the Christians' cruelty. The episode illustrated in this painting is not fully documented as far as the ordeal itself is concerned. Together with Brother Illuminato, Francis had set out from the Christian camp towards the Saracen front, even though he knew that the Sultan had promised a reward of one gold bezant (an ancient gold coin of the Byzantine Empire) to anyone who brought him the head of a Christian. But Francis, mindful of the Gospel passage that says, « I am sending you out to be like sheep among the wolves » (Mt 10,16), reached the Sultan after having first been captured, tied up and beaten by the soldiers. He had a burning desire for martyrdom and he also wanted to convert the Sultan, but neither of these events were to take place because the Sultan refused the trial for fear that he would make a bad impression before his people. In fact, even St. Bonaventure, the famous biographer who wrote the *Major Life* of Francis, fails to discuss this episode. The Sultan, who realized that he was in the presence of a great spirit, did not inveigh against Francis. Instead, he had him escorted back to the Christian camp after having offered him gifts which are now kept in the private sacristy of the Assisi Basilica. Francis refused these gifts at first, but then he finally accepted them upon the great insistence of the Sultan, who marveled at the saint's contempt for worldly goods. Once he had seen how useless it was for him to accept the proposal to stay with the Sultan and his people, and in view of the fact that his desire to die as a martyr of the faith had also been frustrated, Francis decided to return to Italy. Dante recalled this decision in Canto XI of *Paradiso* (100-105):

> When he, in thirst of martyrdom, erect
> stood in the presence of the proud Soldan
> And preached Christ and the band of his elect,
> Seeing the people were too crude a clan
> To be converted, he, not tarrying more,
> Returned to garner ripe Italian grain.

According to a passage in Chapter XXIV of the *Little Flowers*, the Sultan had been converted in secret because he was afraid of showing his people his profound change of heart. Nevertheless, this conversion has no historic foundation but is simply a legendary embellishment that has been believed since the thirteenth century.

QUALITER CUM ALIQUANDO BEATUS FRANCISCUS FERVENTER ORARET VISUS EST A FRATRIBUS TOTO CORPORE SUBLEVATUS A TERRA, MANIBUS PROTEN-SIS, ET NUBECULA QUAEDAM LUCIDISSIMA CIRCUMFULSIT EUM.

How Blessed Francis, as he was praying devotedly, was seen raised up from the ground and surrounded with a shining cloud, and his hands were outstretched in the form of a cross.

[LM X, 4]

12 - Ecstasy of St. Francis

On several occasions we have mentioned Francis' apostolic activity, which essentially became a true social activity. In this painting, however, we see Francis at the height of his mystical activity and the result is that contemplation and action come together within him. His astonished companions look on as their father, in ecstasy, has his arms outstretched in the form of a cross. His entire body is in levitation and has been lifted from the ground as he speaks to Christ, who blesses him from on high. Even the city itself, with its gaping windows, seems to share in the friars' amazement. Francis, however, did not divulge the recondite secrets of divine wisdom unless he felt it was necessary to fulfill a charitable impulse towards his neighbor. He would say that one risked losing a priceless treasure to gain a small reward, since perhaps God would not readily offer a second chance. It is thought that the composition of the scene as well as the architectural formulation on the left were done by Giotto himself. For the most part, however, it seems that the execution of the painting was done by his assistants. The landscape is represented by three simple tress sprouting from a rock.

QUOMODO BEATUS FRANCISCUS IN MEMORIAM NATALIS CHRISTI FECIT PRAEPARARI PRAESEPIUM, APPORTARI FOENUM, BOVEM ET ASINUM ADDUCI, ET DE NATIVITATE PAUPERIS REGIS PRAEDICAVIT, ITEMQUE SANCTO VIRO ORATIONEM HABENTE, MILES QUIDAM VIDIT PUERM IESUM LOCO ILLIUS QUEM SANCTUS ATTULERAT.

How Blessed Francis, in memory of the birth of Christ, had a crib prepared, that hay and that an ox and an ass be brought in, and afterwords he preached to the people about the birth of the poor King. Then a knight saw the Child Jesus in the place of that child placed there by the Saint.

[LM X, 7; 1 Cel. 84-87]

13 - The Crib at Greccio

On Christmas night in 1223, Francis instituted the first living crib in the middle of the woods at Greccio, a town in the province of Rieti. The idea of the crib dates back to more ancient times and was sculpted in bas-reliefs and on sarcophagi, but only with Francis did it become so widespread. Taking artistic license again, Giotto imagined that this event took place inside a church that some have described as Romanesque and that could even be the Lower Church itself. On the other hand, some critics retain that it was the church in the castle at Greccio. The Assisi Basilica could be recognized by the rood-screen and by the backside of the wooden Crucifix stretching out over the nave, which is presumably quite large and packed with worshippers. The purpose of this crucifix is to act as a real « transmitter » of the idea of space. Other details worthy of mention include the Arnolfo ciborium, the lectern and the way the steps converge into a marvelous compositional unity accentuating the definition of space. Note the ox and ass, tiny with respect to the height of the characters: these animals show the humble yet necessary presence of nature. Francis himself is wearing a deacon's robe. Since Francis wanted to commemorate the birth of Jesus, to meditate and to make others meditate on the great mystery of the incarnation of God, he invited so many people, together with his friars, that the forests of Greccio resounded with their voices and were illuminated with a multitude of bright lights. St. Bonaventure recounts that « the saint stood before the crib and his great heart overflowed with tender compassion; he was bathed in tears but overcome with joy. » The solemnities of the Mass were celebrated over the manger and Francis sang the Gospel and preached the mystery of the Nativity, lovingly calling Christ "the Child of Bethlehem". Giovanni Velita, a knight from Greccio who had taken charge of all the preparations and a trustworthy man of exemplary virtue, related that he saw a small child asleep in the crib and that Francis took him in his arms and seemed to wake him up. His joyous heart was undoubtedly in Bethlehem. Francis' crib is not a crib reflecting the "propaganda of poverty" as we twentieth-century men understand it. Instead, it was a spontaneous contact with the little things, with that special mystery, with that small yet great story that is told through the emotions and the symbols of Christian life.

CUM BEATUS FRANCISCUS CAUSA INFIRMITATIS IN ASINO UNIUS PAUPERIS HOMINIS ASCENDERET QUEMDAM MONTEM, EIDEM HOMINI SITI PERICLITANTI ORANDO AQUAM PRODUXIT DE PETRA, QUAE NEC ANTEA FUERAT NEC POSTEA VISA EST.

When Blessed Francis, because he was weak, rode up the mountainside on an ass belonging to a poor laborer. For this same man, who was fainting with thirst, Francis started to pray, and he made water spring forth from the rock. Water had never been found at that spot before, and none could ever be found there afterwards. [LM VII, 12; 2 Cel. 46]

14 - Miracle of the spring

This fresco is unanimously considered to be one of the finest paintings in the Assisi cycle and only part of it was done by Giotto himself. Nevertheless, the artistic conception was entirely his own. The scene depicts Francis who, while on his way to Mount La Verna to dedicate himself to contemplation, made water spring forth from a rock to quench the thirst of a poor local man. The man had offered Francis his donkey to spare him the strenuous climb, as Francis was quite ill and weak. The man followed Francis through the hills on foot, but at a certain point, he began to complain that he was very thirsty and he even cried out, « I'm dying of thirst. I'll die if I don't get a drink immediately. » So Francis promptly dismounted from the donkey and knelt down to pray. In answer to his prayer, Christ let the man drink the water that gushed from solid stone. Not even the tiniest stream had ever been found there before, and none could be found there afterwards. A parallel is being drawn here between Francis and Moses, who had also made water flow from a rock. The planes and outlines of the rocks correspond precisely to the positions of the single groups of figures. The two friars on the left are vertical, just as the rock behind them is vertical; Francis is bending forward, following the slope of the mountain; the thirsty man is horizontal, just as the rock on which he is lying is also horizontal. The figures look as if they were sculpted on the arid rock, while the donkey adds a delicately poetic note. The triangular blue patch of sky penetrates the massive bulk of the mountains, a characteristic we already noted in the second fresco. The trees sprouting from the rock lend even greater emphasis to the dryness of the rock. Here too we are able to observe Giotto's eloquent idea that shows the two groups united in the center by the dominating figure of the Saint, who has a direct relationship with God. The painting was cleaned completely in 1978 because humidity had caused extensive damage.

CUM BEATUS FRANCISCUS IRET BEVANIUM PRAEDICAVIT MULTIS AVIBUS QUAE GES-
TIENTES EXTENDEBANT COLLA, PROTENDEBANT ALAS, APERIEBANT ROSTRA, TUNI-
CAM EIUS TANGEBANT, ET ISTA OMNIA VIDEBANT SOCII EXPECTANTES IN VIA.

How Blessed Francis, on his way to Bevagna, started to preach to many birds that joyfully stretched
out their necks, flapped their wings, opened their beaks and even pecked at his habit. His companions who were waiting on the road saw everything. [LM XII, 3; 1 Cel. 58; LF XVI]

15 - Sermon to the birds

This episode took place in the fields of Pian d'Arca, about a half-hour walk from Bevagna, perhaps between 1212 and 1213. There is now a modern building on this site to commemorate this extraordinary event. This fresco is one of the most famous and most often reproduced paintings of the entire Giotto cycle. The extremely compact three-dimensional space is obtained through the juxtaposition of the curvature of the horizon and the slight inclination of the tree trunks on the right and on the left. The foliage of the two trees is then isolated in the blue sky. In this scene, Francis is talking to the animals and for the moment, his interest no longer lies in God or man, but in Nature. This is the famous triad of the Franciscan message that Giotto has portrayed in this cycle with masterly skill: the Creator, His creatures, Creation. This is a new aspect of Francis' holiness: just look at the astonishment expressed by Brother Masseo (Brother Giacomo of Massa was also there during this event, but he is not shown in the painting). Look at his right hand, which is raised as if to say that such an attitude had never been seen before in a saint. Prior to Giotto, animals were represented as mere symbols or as simple decorations, but here animals become a presence that can converse with man and like man, they are protagonists in the life of the world. Now the *Canticle of the Creatures* is strongly evoked, because Francis urged all things living and inanimate to praise their Creator. No one ever raised a greater hymn to the « material » element of the cosmos than Francis did in his *Canticle of Brother Sun*. It marks the beginning of vernacular Italian and has been understood and must always be understood as an original score. Francis is the great director who, with his right arm raised, seems to start the opening notes of the magnificent symphony of creation. Let us recall how Francis always recounted this event to his friars with great joy in his heart. He described how huge flocks of birds of every kind (including doves, magpies, avocets and crows) came so close to him that they didn't even move when he brushed against them with his habit. He told his friars how the birds stretched out their necks, spread their little wings, opened their beaks and attentively set their eyes on him. Only after they had heard Francis' words and had been given his blessing did they fly up in the shape of the Cross, going off into four different directions. According to the « Franciscan Sources, » Francis addressed them with these words: « My brother birds, you should praise your Creator very much because he clothed you with feathers and gave you wings to fly, appointing the clear air as your home, and he looks after you without any effort on your part. He gave you rivers and springs to drink from, mountains and valleys as your refuges and trees in which to make your nests. Always be careful not to be ungrateful. » This episode can be interpreted symbolically. The flight of the birds in a cross formation represents the diaspora of the friars throughout the world to teach people about the Cross and to exhort them to trust only in divine Providence, just as the birds of the air do. The painting has also been interpreted by positivistic critics as a sort of reappraisal of Francis' personality. These critics see Francis as the « long hand » of the Vatican or as an *instrumentum regni* of the papacy. It has been purported that since animals represent the mute part of Creation, the part most subjugated and violated by man, Francis' sermon is offered merely to pacify the populace that works, suffers and is exploited and outraged. This interpretation, like the previous ones, fails automatically because Francis had no desire to coerce nor to pacify anyone. In fact, he blessed the birds, who were then free to fly to the four corners of the earth. There are some faded areas on some of the birds where they had been touched up « a secco. »

CUM BEATUS FRANCISCUS IMPETRAVIT SALUTEM ANIMAE CUIDAM MILITI DE CELANO QUI EUM DEVOTE AD PRANDIUM INVITAVERAT, QUI ET POST CONFESSIONEM ET DOMUS SUAE DISPOSITIONEM ALIIS MANDUCARE INCIPIENTIBUS, IPSE STATIM SPIRITUM EXHALAVIT ET IN DOMINO OBDORMIVIT

When Blessed Francis saved the soul of a certain knight of Celano, who out of humble devotion had invited him to lunch. After he confessed and had put his house in order, as the others began to eat, he suddenly breathed forth his spirit and passed away.

[LM XI, 4; 3 Cel. 41]

16 - Death of the knight of Celano

The Franciscan Sources relate that after Francis returned from overseas, he went to preach in Celano d'Abruzzo. There, with his devout prayers and much insistence, a knight invited him and his companions to dine at his house. It is thought that this knight may even have been a relative of Brother Tommaso of Celano, who later became Francis' first biographer. Before the meal, Francis offered prayers and praise to God. Then he gently took his kind host aside to tell him to make his confession immediately, for that very day, the Lord was to reward him for having welcomed the « Poverello » of God and his poor followers so devoutly into his home. Thus, the knight prepared for death by confessing his sins and putting his house in order and then he passed away at peace with God and man. This episode could refer to a passage from the Gospel according to Matthew (10,41), which says, « He who welcomes a prophet... receives a prophet's reward. » In other words, the knight will receive the same reward in heaven that Francis will receive. However, we could also interpret this passage differently and perhaps more correctly if we consider it to mean that anyone who welcomes a prophet will receive the reward a prophet can give and that is, the chance to prepare for imminent death in order to save one's soul in time. In this painting, Francis is truly the prophet of Christ and the herald of God. In fact, from this painting on, Francis' portrayal as the *alter Christus*, or « other Christ » takes on greater substance, in accordance with the paintings in the upper registers of this wall that illustrate the life of Christ. In essence, because of the Stigmata he received, Francis is similar to Christ and consequently, all creatures obey him since he is thoroughly aware of the common origin of all things. From an aesthetic point of view, the painting is one of the most accomplished examples of Giotto's dramatic composition. The laid but deserted table is set off against the anonymous group of agitated women wailing over the dying knight. The astonished yet calm look of the friar seated at the table, who nevertheless has faith in Francis' cognizant actions, contrasts sharply with the commotion among the family members gathered around the dying man. As in the fifth fresco, these two groups differ numerically as well, but they are connected by Francis' gaze and by the look given to him by the man in red. The building is decorated with cosmatesgue ne work and even it alone confers greater importance to the figure of the Saint, who is placed almost inside the jutting niche. Unlike what will be done in Renaissance painting, the perspective here has no vanishing point. It is composed using lines that appear to be parallel but that are actually oblique. An example of this can be seen in the short ends of the table.

CUM BEATUS FRANCISCUS CORAM DOMINO PAPA ET CARDINALIBUS ITA DE-
VOTE ET EFFICACITER PRAEDICAVIT, UT PATENTER CLARESCERET QUOD IP-
SE NON IN DOCTIS HUMANAE SAPIENTIAE VERBIS SED DIVINO SPIRITU LO-
QUERETUR.

When Blessed Francis, in the presence of the Lord Pope and of the Cardinals, offered a
sermon that was so eloquent it was clear that he did not speak with learned words of human
wisdom, but divinely inspired by God.

[LM XII, 7; 1 Cel. 73; Sab. XIV]

17 - Francis preaching before Honorius III

This fresco depicts Francis' sermon before Honorius III, the pope who succeeded Innocent III. This sermon was inspired by divine revelation. We must start by saying that by this time, the Franciscan Order was very widespread (it is now the year 1223). Francis was already thinking of asking the new pope to confirm the « way of life » that had been approved orally by Innocent III in 1209 and that had later been rewritten by the friars so it could be presented at the Chapter of 1221. Then Francis had a vision. On the ground he saw innumerable tiny crumbs of bread to be distributed to a multitude of friars, but the Saint feared that since these crumbs were so small, they would slip through his fingers. So a voice from heaven said to him, « Make of these crumbs a single host and offer it to anyone who wishes to eat of it. » Francis did as he was told, but he realized that those who did not receive that gift devoutly or who, after having received it, were contemptuous of it, immediately appeared to be infected with leprosy. Francis did not understand the meaning of this revelation but a voice from heaven said to him, « Francis, the crumbs of last night are the words of the Gospel, the host is the Rule, the leprosy is wickedness. » He therefore decided to condense the Rule that, with the help of Brother Cesario da Spira, he had elaborated based on the Rule of 1209. As we already mentioned, the new Rule was to be presented at the Chapter of 1221. The Rule of 1209, called the *Regula prima*, or « First Rule, » had been too lengthy. Therefore, together with Brother Leone and Brother Bonizio, Francis retreated to a mountain in the Rieti Valley that is now known as Fonte colombo but which was called Mount Rainerio at that time. Praying and fasting, he drew up the new Rule, which he entrusted to his Vicar, Brother Elia of Cortona. He then went to Rome to make his request to the Pope. He had memorized a speech, but when it was time to give it, he completely forgot it. Invoking the grace of the Holy Spirit, his words then flowed with such eloquence that even the Papal Court itself realized that it was not Francis who spoke but the Spirit of the Lord. With his papal Bull *Solet annuere* of November 29, 1223, Honorius III approved what was called the *Regula secunda* or *Bullata* [Second or Sealed Rule]. However, the canons of the Curia had restructured the Rule to give it a juridical form. Because of this, several Franciscan historians have said that the Church of Rome took over the Order, absorbing it into its own system as it had done with the Dominican Rule. Incidentally, we quote here the words Paul Sabatier wrote in Chapter XIII of his *Life of St. Francis of Assisi*: « ... just as the fraternity instituted by Francis was truly the fruit of his body, flesh of his flesh, so does the Order of the Preaching Friars emanate from the Papacy and St. Dominic is only its putative father. » Consequently, while there is a profound difference between the two founders, the work of the Curia is aimed instead towards a single objective in these two cases and that is, to « protect » both Orders. In Canto XI of *Paradiso* (91-108), Dante refers to the Rule as « the first signet, » connoting the approval of Innocent III. Then he refers to the « second wreath, » or the Eternal Spirit that acted within Honorius III, and lastly he mentions « the final imprint, » or the Stigmata given to Francis by Christ on Mount La Verna. Getting back to Giotto's fresco, notice the spatial arrangement, taken from the plan of the Upper Church, the Gothic architecture of the façade, and the throne, decorated with cosmatesque work, which is foreshortened to place greater emphasis on the characters themselves. Other details worthy of note include the various postures of the members of the Curia, not to mention the Pope's deep concentration, which is reflected in his sharp and intelligent gaze. This is thought to be a portrait of Boniface VIII, who was Pope at the time Giotto did these frescoes.

CUM BEATUS ANTONIUS IN CAPITULO ARELATENSI DE TITULO CRUCIS PRAEDICARET, BEATUS FRANCISCUS ABSENS CORPORE APPARUIT, ET EXTENSIS MANIBUS, BENEDIXIT FRATRES, SICUT VIDIT QUIDAM FRATER MONALDUS, ET ALII FRATRES CONSOLATIONEM MAXIMAM HABUERUNT.

While Blessed Anthony was preaching at the Chapter of Arles on the inscription at the top of the Cross, Blessed Francis, who was not present, appeared bodily with his arms outstretched and blessed his brothers. This is what a certain Monaldo saw and all the other brothers were filled with great consolation.

[LM IV, 10; 1 Cel. 48; 3 Cel. 3]

18 - Apparition at Arles

The scene is set inside an austere capitular hall in the city of Arles, in Provence. The friars have been convened to a chapter meeting by St. Anthony of Padua who, contrary to how he may appear, is not fat but swollen because he was afflicted with dropsy. Just as Jesus had appeared to his disciples behind closed doors on the third day of His Resurrection, Francis, who never went to France in person, appeared with his arms upraised in the form of a Cross, almost as if to transform this stern meeting into a true fraternal festivity. This episodes attests to just one of Francis' many paranormal faculties and that is, his power to appear in two places at once, an event reported in great detail in the "Franciscan Sources". According to these sources, as St. Anthony was discussing the meaning of the inscription « INRI » written on the scroll at the top of the Cross, Brother Monaldo saw Francis with his very own eyes. Francis was hovering in the air as he blessed the friars and all of them were pervaded with a feeling of extraordinary spiritual consolation. The provincial Chapter of Arles was held in 1224 under the leadership of St. Anthony, who was born in Lisbon and entered the Franciscan Order in 1220. St. Anthony had already participated in the famous « Chapter of Mats » held in 1221 in the square of Santa Maria degli Angeli around the Porziuncola. That chapter was attended by 3000 friars, although some sources claim that 5000 friars were present. He was still alive when Tommaso of Celano mentioned him in his biography of St. Francis. He died in 1231 at the age of 36, five years after Francis' death and was canonized within one year. Note the architectonic function of Francis' open arms, which contrast with the ogival arches in the background. The entire fresco is thought to have been conceived by Giotto but he supposedly frescoed only the figure of St. Anthony, leaving the rest to his assistants.

CUM BEATUS FRANCISCUS ORARET IN LATERE MONTIS ALVERNAE, VIDIT CHRISTUM IN SPECIE SERAPHIM CRUCIFIXI, QUI IMPRESSIT IN MANIBUS ET PEDIBUS ET ETIAM IN LATERE DEXTRO STIGMATA CRUCIS EIUSDEM DOMINI NOSTRI IESU CHRISTI.

While Blessed Francis was praying on the side of Mount La Verna, he had a vision of Christ, under the guise of a crucified Seraph. The Seraph impressed the Stigmata of the Cross on his hands, his feet and even his right side. They were the same ones born by Our Lord Jesus Christ.

[LM XIII, 3; 1 Cel. 94, 95]

19 - The Stigmata

This scene has inspired innumerable artistic variations over the centuries. Mount La Verna (could this be an abbreviation of Mons *Cavernae*), located in the Casentine Valley, was donated to Francis by Count Orlando Cattani of Chiusi of La Verna as early as 1213. Francis had already stayed there on numerous occasions and extraordinary episodes had taken place there many times. In the early hours of September 15, 1224, as Francis was praying in a secluded spot on the mountainside, he saw a Seraph with six resplendent fiery wings come down from the heavens. The Seraph had two wings at his shoulders, two at his sides and two on his legs. In the middle of his wings was the image of a crucified man and Francis was astounded because as he well knew, the agony of the Passion is completely inconsistent with the beatitude of a seraph. However, he finally understood that God was announcing to him the complete transformation that his body was about to undergo and that would assimilate him to the Crucified Christ. The six wings of the Seraph could represent the six steps that lead the mind to perfect illumination. On the other hand, they could also be the six symbolic steps of Solomon's throne, or in other words, the path leading to supreme wisdom and to the sublime peace of God. As St. Bonaventure said in his *Itinerarium mentis in Deum*, this will take place when the mind can see « joined together the First and Last, the infinite and the divine, the center and the circumference, alpha and omega, cause and effect, the creature and his Creator. » When the vision disappeared, the marks of the nails began to appear in Francis' hands and feet. His right side was also covered with a red wound that often bled, staining his tunic and his trousers so much that his garments had to be lengthened to cover his chest. Through the Stigmata, Francis was identified with Christ not only just spiritually but physically now as well. For him, La Verna was the indeed the Mount Tabor of his transfiguration, but it was also the Golgotha of his suffering. In Canto XI of *Paradiso* (106-108), Dante wrote:

> On the rough rock 'twixt Tiber and Arno shore
> He took that final imprint of the rood
> From Christ, which for two years his body bore.

It would take too long for us to discuss the phenomenon of the Stigmata here. Suffice it to say that Francis' Stigmata were not only the most famous in the history of Christianity, but they were also the first, since subsequently there were reports of at least 300 cases of stigmatization, although not all of them could be verified. In Francis' case, the so-called 'Assisi parchment' lists the names of sixteen witnesses who saw and touched Francis' Stigmata following his death. The name of the nobleman Girolamo of Assisi should also be added to this list (see fresco 22). The cardinals who witnessed the truth of the Stigmata included Ugolino of the Counts of Segni, Tommaso of Capua, Raniero Capocci of Viterbo and Stefano of Casanuova, and these men composed some of the hymns and antiphons used in the liturgical Office for Francis. Francis always kept the Stigmata covered as much as possible, but Brother Leone as well as Brother Rufino di Scipione, St. Clare's cousin, were permitted to see the wound in his side. It was Brother Elia, vicar of the Order, who announced to the Order and to the world that Francis had received the Stigmata and now for the first time, people began to speak of the Saint as the new Crucified. The image of the Seraph has become very dim. The figure on the right may have been done by an assistant. On the rock to the left, there are traces of flowers and small plants that were painted « a secco » or on dry plaster.

*QUOMODO IN HORA TRANSITUS BEATI FRANCISCI UNUS FRATER VIDIT ANI-
MAM EIUS SUB SPECIE STELLAE PRAEFULGIDAE IN COELUM ASCENDERE.*

How at the hour of the death of Blessed Francis, one of the friars saw his soul ascend into
heaven under the appearance of a radiant star.

[LM XIV, 6; 1 Cel. 8; 2 Cel. 214-217; 3 Cel. 37-39]

20 - Death of St. Francis

Francis wanted to return to the Porziuncola so he could die in the place known today as the Chapel of the Transitus. At that time, it served as an infirmary for the friars. He wanted to die, not in Assisi where he had received only physical life, but at the place in which he had received true life. It was the evening of October 3, 1226 and a flock of skylarks, birds that usually love daylight and abhor darkness, circled festively over the rooftop nevertheless. It was here that all God's designs were fulfilled in Francis. As he took leave of this world, he told his friars to love poverty always and to do their part as he had done his. He then imparted his blessing to each one of them, just as the patriarch Jacob had blessed his sons long ago. « He stretched his right hand over them and starting with his vicar [Broter Elia], he placed it on each one's head. » Then he asked the friars to chant the prayer that David recited when he was in the cave, the 142nd psalm. It begins, « With a loud voice I cry out to the Lord » and then ends with the invocation, « Lead me forth from prison. » One of his disciples saw Francis' soul, under the appearance of a radiant star, being borne on a white cloud and going straight to heaven. In this fresco, we see the saint's body stretched out on a wooden table. Above it is the image of Francis who, poor and humble on earth, is rich and glorious as he enters heaven carried by angels. After his death, his body was brought into the little church of St. George, which today is a chapel inside the Basilica of Santa Chiara. It remained there for three years and eight months until it was transferred to the new Basilica on May 25, 1230. Francis' original burial place is still the subject of great debate. In fact, while some say it was the actual Chapel of St. George, others sustain that it was the Chapel of St. Francis in the cloister-garden of the early monastery of the Poor Clares and still others say it was the crypt beneath the Church of St. George, a large quadrangular room that the nuns call « Sottosanti » (« under the saints »). Although it may have seemed to be the most logical solution, Francis was not buried in the Porziuncola. Because of its isolated position in the open countryside, it was more readily exposed to the danger of theft, especially by the people of Perugia. The death of St. Francis is commemorated on October 4th, because according to a medieval custom that remained part of the liturgy, the day was calculated from one vesper (sunset) to the next, rather than from midnight to midnight as we do today. Francis died on the evening of October 3rd after vespers and consequently, his feastday was established on the following day, October 4th. The "Franciscan Sources" relate that Brother Elias, who signed himself « vile sinner » and « the weak and lowliest servant of the Friars Minor, » sent an encyclical to all the Provinces of the Order to express the grief they shared over the death of their « Father » and to announce that Francis bore five wounds on his body, the true Stigmata of Christ. Brother Elia's letter is interlaced with biblical quotations and with allusions to Jacob, Moses, Aaron and John the Baptist. This fresco is located beneath the « Crucifixion of Christ » depicted in the upper registers, thus bearing further witness to Francis' *conformitas to Christ*.

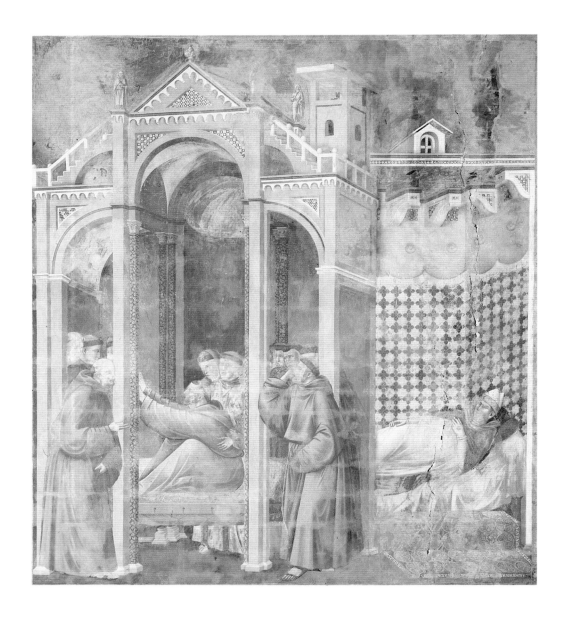

MINISTER TERRAE LABORIS CUM LABORARET IN EXTREMIS ET DIU IAM PERDIDISSET LOQUELAM, CLAMAVIT ET DIXIT: EXPECTA ME, PATER, ECCE VENIO TECUM ET STA-TIM DEFUNCTUS SECUTUS EST SANCTUM PATREM. EPISCOPUS INSUPER ASSISII CUM ESSET IN MONTE SANCTI MICHAELIS ARCHANGELI VIDIT BEATUM FRANCISCUM DI-CENTEM SIBI: ECCE VADO AD COELUM. ET TALI HORA ITA INVENTUM EST.

A minister in « Terra di Lavoro », at his last hour and long without the faculty of speech, began to cry out, saying, « Wait for me Father. I am coming with you. » He died then and there and followed his holy father. At the same time, the Bishop of Assisi, who was at the mountain of St. Michael the Archangel, had a vision of Blessed Francis who said to him, « Behold, I am going to heaven. » And in fact this occurred at the very same hour.   [LM IV, 6; 2 Cel. 218, 220]

21 - Apparition to Brother Agostino and Bishop Guido

On the very night of his death, Francis appeared to Bishop Guido of Assisi, who was on a pilgrimage to the Shrine of St. Michael the Archangel on Mount Gargano, saying to him, « Behold, I am leaving the world and I'm going to heaven, » just as Christ had said to his disciples (John 16,28). Francis also appeared to Brother Augustino, provincial minister of the brothers in « Terra di Lavoro » (this province covered the south-central region of Campania in the area known as *felix*, which extended from just north of Naples almost to the Liri River, although according to other sources, it covered the region of Apulia). This brother, an upright and holy man who had lost the power of speech long before, was now on his deathbed. All those present heard him exclaim, « Wait for me, father, wait! Behold, I am coming with you. » Then, addressing the amazed people around him, he added, « Can't you see our father Francis? He is going up to heaven. » And shortly thereafter he passed away. Christ's words to the good thief immediately come to mind: « This day, you will be with me in paradise » (Lk 23,43). Art historian Edi Baccheschi notes that « the entire painting is thought to be the work of assistants and even the conception of the scene appears to be foreign to Giotto's spatial concepts. »

IN PORTIUNCULA ET CUM IACERET BEATUS FRANCISCUS MORTUUS, DOMI-NUS HIERONYMUS DOCTOR ET LITTERATUS CELEBER MOVEBAT CLAVOS SANCTIQUE MANUS, PEDES ET LATUS MANIBUS PROPRIIS CONTRECTABAT.

While Blessed Francis lay dead at the Porziuncola, the knight Girolamo, a famous doctor and man of letters, moved the nails [of the Stigmata] and felt the Saint's hands, feet and side with his own hand.

[LM XV, 4]

22 - Verification of the Stigmata

While Francis' body was being moved from the Porziuncola to the Chapel of St. George, an incredulous nobleman named Girolamo, a learned man who was a judge and administrator in the Comune of Assisi, stopped the funeral cortege so he could inspect the Stigmata in person. After he had done so, he swore to their authenticity on the Bible. As we can see, out of respect for the Saint, he placed his hat on the ground to the left. This is yet another episode that is part of the parallels drawn between the life of Christ and the life of Francis and in fact, it recalls Thomas' skepticism about Christ's wounds. In the upper part of the scene is the cross that actually did hang in the nave of the Upper Church, which is where Giotto, taking artistic license yet again, has set this scene. The cross is the famous Crucifix Brother Elia commissioned to Giunta Pisano in 1236 and that was lost toward the end of the seventeenth century. (It is possible that Brother Elia also commissioned Giunta Pisano to do the small Crucifix that was to be hung in the Porziuncola and that is now displayed in the Museum of Santa Maria degli Angeli.) Hanging next to the Crucifix are images depicting the Madonna with Child and Michael the Archangel. The characteristic pulley-type chandelier, which can be raised or lowered using the hanging rope, also deserves mention. This fresco is interesting from an aesthetic viewpoint in that the characters are portrayed in profile. One of the characters is even shown from behind, an idea that would have been unthinkable in the Byzantine tradition. Instead, Giotto even goes to the point of « twisting » the figure around completely.

CUM TURBAE QUAE CONVENERANT DEFERRENT AD CIVITATEM ASSISII CUM RAMIS ARBORUM ET CEREORUM MULTIPLICATIS LUMINIBUS SACRUM COR-PUS MARGARITIS COELESTIBUS INSIGNITUM, EUM VIDENDUM BEATAE CLA-RAE ET ALIIS SACRIS VIRGINIBUS OBTULERUNT.

How the crowd from the city of Assisi had assembled, taking up branches from the trees and bearing a multitude of candles, and carried the sacred body adorned with the Stigmata like celestial pearls so that Blessed Clare and her virgin sisters could see him.

[LM XV, 5; 1 Cel. 116-118]

23 - Mourning of the Clares

One of the most beautiful and fascinating paintings of this cycle, this fresco portrays Clare and her companions, known at that time as the « Poor Sisters of San Damiano » or "Damianites", as they bid their final farewell to their deceased Master and Father. We know that the Poor Clares were and still are cloistered religious. Thus they could not have left their convent, something which Giotto instead imagines was possible. This is another example of Giotto's artistic license. Yet another example of this can be seen in the façade of the church, which certainly cannot be the church of San Damiano, a poor rustic oratory even today. Giotto depicts it instead as a richly decorated church with cresting, niches and an eagle on top of the gable. The man, or boy, who is climbing the tree to see the passage of the alter Christus, adds a quaint touch. This character is reminiscent of Zacchaeus, who climbed the sycamore to see Jesus when He passed by (Lk 19, 1-10). It is traditionally said that Clare tried to tear the so-called « nails » of the Stigmata from the saint's hands and that fresh blood spurted forth instead. Giotto portrayed Saint Clare with a halo, just as he had done with Francis in the first panel, because at the time these paintings were done, both Francis and Clare had already been canonized. According to the " Franciscan Sources ", while Francis' holy body was being carried from the Porziuncola to Assisi, the procession stopped momentarily before the little church of San Damiano so that Clare could see him for the last time. For this reason, the little grate through which the Poor Clares received the Eucharist was opened. The litter was carried over to Clare, and her spiritual daughters wept and wailed when they saw their father, who would no longer speak to them. The « Sources » proceed to say that « divided between sorrow and joy, they kissed his most radiant hands, adorned with [the Stigmata glowing like] shining pearls ». The historic grate was later moved from San Damiano to the present-day basilica in Assisi that was built in 1260 in Clare's honor. The funeral procession then continued on to the church of St. George in Assisi, where the body of St. Francis remained from October 4, 1226 until May 25, 1230. It was then moved to the great Basilica built by Brother Elia. The execution of this painting has been attributed almost unanimously to Giotto's assistants. However, the fresco is based on Giotto's own idea.

CUM DOMINUS PAPA PERSONALITER VENIENS AD CIVITATEM ASSISIO, MIRA-
CULIS DILIGENTER DISCUSSIS, DE CONSILIO FRATRUM SUORUM BEATUM
FRANCISCUM CANONIZAVIT ET CATALOGO SANCTORUM ASCRIPSIT.

How the Pope, who went to the city of Assisi in person after having carefully discussed the
miracles and with the deliberation of his brothers, canonized Blessed Francis and inscribed his name in the catalogue of saints.

[LM XV, 7; 1 Cel. 123-126]

From this fresco through the twenty-eighth one, critics have attributed the work either to Giotto's disciples or to the St. Cecilia Master, so named because of the painting he did depicting scenes from the life of St. Cecilia, a work now kept in the Uffizi Gallery in Florence. Even as early as the twentieth fresco, however, Giotto's participation was beginning to be less and less frequent. Giotto had left Assisi to go to Rome, as Boniface VIII had summoned him to paint a fresco in the loggia of the Lateran Basilica in honor of the first jubilee year of Christianity that the pope had proclaimed for the year 1300. With the exception of a central fragment that is now preserved inside the basilica, that fresco has since been lost. The panel we are now admiring, which unfortunately has undergone extensive damage because vast areas of color have fallen, represents the canonization of Francis. This event took place in the open air outside the little church of St. George in Assisi on Sunday, July 16, 1228. On that day, Gregory IX inscribed Francis' name in the catalogue of saints, to the great joy of all the clergy and the faithful in attendance. Both Tommaso of Celano and St. Bonaventure offer a very detailed description of the canonization ceremony, even including parts of the ritual prayers that were said. Among those present was Giovanni I of Brienne, who had been crowned King of Jerusalem in 1210 and who later became a Friar Minor; he is buried in the Basilica in Assisi. The day after the canonization, Gregory IX himself lay the first stone of the basilica that was to be built in Francis' honor as his sepulcher through the centuries. In his Bull *Recolentes* of April 29, 1228, Pope Gregory had already asked Christians to contribute toward the construction of a « special church. » On April 22, 1230, a mere twenty-two months after he had laid the foundation-stone, Gregory IX declared in his Bull *Is qui ecclesia* that this church was *caput et mater* (head and mother) of the Franciscan Order and he requested that Francis' body be translated from the little church of St. George to « Colle del Paradiso » (Paradise Hill), which had formerly been known as « Colle dell'Inferno » (Hell Hill). In this same Bull, Gregory IX invited Christians from all over Europe to participate in the translation of Francis' sacred remains. This ceremony was held on May 25, 1230, the same year in which the friars held their general chapter in Assisi. To the sound of trumpets and other musical instruments, Francis' body was placed on a richly decorated wagon that was drawn by oxen draped in purple and escorted by armed guards and soldiers. The Saint's tomb was later rediscovered in 1818. It was found beneath the main altar, where Brother Elia had placed it in 1230. Francis' canonization would have been celebrated in Rome; however due to popular rebellions instigated by Frederick II, Gregory IX had been forced to flee the city to seek refuge in Rieti, Spoleto and finally in Perugia for several months. Frederick had been excommunicated by Pope Gregory for having simulated a crusade that in fact had never taken place. But the glorification most worthy of Francis was the one celebrated by the skylarks with their joyous flight over the roof of the Porziuncola. This was a glorification that the Saint could never have imagined and it was the most spontaneous and immediate of all — nature's true celebration in his honor. In the lower right-hand corner of the fresco, there is a lady fiddling with a child's hair, a detail that would have been inconceivable in Byzantine art. Nevertheless, by now the pictorial language seen here is quite removed from Giotto.

CUM DOMINUS PAPA GREGORIUS ALIQUANTULUM DUBITARET DE PLAGA VULNERIS LATERALIS, DIXIT EI IN SOMNIS BEATUS FRANCISCUS: DA MIHI PHIALAM VACUAM, QUAM CUM SIBI DARET, SANGUINIS LATERIS VIDEBATUR IMPLERI.

When the Pope was rather doubtful about the wound in Francis' side, Blessed Francis appeared to him in a dream and said to him, « Give me an empty phial ». Having given it to him, he saw that it was filled with blood from his side.

[LM, Miracles I, 2]

25 - Dream of Gregory IX

This is the first fresco in the final group of four frescoes concerning Francis' miracles. In this panel, we see Francis' apparition to Gregory IX, the former Cardinal Ugolino of the Counts of Segni, whom Francis had chosen as « corrector and protector » of his Order and whose election to St. Peter's See he had predicted. Gregory IX is the pope who submitted Francis' miracles to be examined by a group of cardinals whose views seemed to be somewhat favorable. After he had obtained a positive response from them, he went to Assisi to proceed with Francis' canonization. In spite of all this, however, the pope was tormented with doubt over the wound in Francis' side because although he had heard about it, he had never actually seen it. In this apparition, however, we see Francis as he raised his right arm to show his wound. He then asked the pope for an empty phial to catch the blood flowing from his side. The Pontiff brought him the phial he had requested and it seemed to fill up to the brim with blood. After this episode, the Pope became a convinced supporter and fervent defender of Francis' Stigmata. It is interesting to note the distinct positions of the four characters in the foreground, who represent three clear-cut human situations: sleep, drowsiness and wakefulness. In fact, the man on the right is sleeping soundly and, as a result, he is excluded from the scene. The two in the center seem to have been awakened just a short time before, whereas the fourth character on the left is the most vigilant of all and is praying. The conception of this panel can undoubtedly be attributed to Giotto, but according to most scholars, any direct participation by him in its actual execution is to be excluded. Art historian Decio Gioseffi was the first to note the use here of frontal asymmetry, a characteristic that became increasingly more common in later cycles done by Giotto in the Arena Chapel in Padua and in the Bardi Chapel in Florence.

BEATUS FRANCISCUS IOANNEM, DE CIVITATE YLERDA, VULNERATUM AD MORTEM ET A MEDICIS DESPERATUM, ET SE, DUM VULNERARETUR, DEVOTE INVOCANTEM, STATIM PERFECTISSIME LIBERAVIT, SACRIS SUIS MANIBUS LIGATURAS SOLVENS ET PLAGAS SUAVISSIME TANGENS.

Blessed Francis, unwinding the bandages with his hands and delicately touching the wounds, immediately and completely cured Giovanni of the city of Lerida who, mortally wounded and given up for dead by the doctors, had devoutly invoked Francis while he was being attacked.

[LM, Miracles I, 5; 3 Cel. 11-13]

26 - Healing of the Man of Lerida

In this fresco, we see Francis, assisted by two angels, as he heals the gentleman of Lerida, Giovanni di Castro, who had been mortally wounded in an ambush. Many of the details in Thomas of Celano's account of this episode differ with respect to St. Bonaventure's. Here we will mention just the location of the city in which the miracle took place. Celano speaks of the kingdom of Castille, whereas St. Bonaventure speaks of Lerida of Aragon. Lerida, which is the ancient city of Ilerda, was conquered in 49 B.C. by Julius Caesar, who had defeated Pompey: this city is in Catalonia. However, the references to Castille and Aragon could mean the same thing, since Aragon was united with the county of Catalonia in 1137 and Castille changed its borders many times throughout history. One evening, Giovanni di Castro, a devout and God-fearing man, was traveling along a road on which an ambush had been prepared. Although he had no enemies, he very closely resembled the man the ambushers planned to kill and this was the cause of the tragedy that left him on the ground, half-dead. It was impossible to cure him because of the number of wounds and injuries he had received. Furthermore, gangrene had set in and his stench was unbearable. All alone in his miserable bed, he prayed to Francis with immense devotion. Suddenly, he saw a man dressed as a Friar Minor enter through the window and stand next to him. The man said to him, « Giovanni you have had confidence in me and so God will save you. » And when Francis' stigmatized hands touched him, John was completely restored to health. We are reminded here of the words spoken by Christ: « Your faith has saved you. » No one would believe the miracle, not even John's wife herself, who had thought that she would be burying him the next day. Nevertheless, Francis bore on his body the same wounds borne by Christ, who with his wounds had healed all mankind, left « wounded and half-dead » (Lk 10,30). Thus, Francis had within him the divine power to work any miracle. Critics have unanimously attributed this painting to the St. Cecilia Master.

BEATUS FRANCISCUS SUSCITAVIT ISTAM DOMINAM MORTUAM QUAE, FACTA CONFESSIONE UNIUS PECCATI QUOD NONDUM FUERAT CONFESSA, VIDENTIBUS CLERICIS ET ALIIS QUI ASTITERUNT, ET ITERUM DEFUNCTA OBDORMIVIT IN DOMINO ET DIABOLUS CONFUSUS AUFUGIT.

Blessed Francis raised this woman from the dead and after she had confessed the only sin she had not previously confessed, beneath the eyes of the clerics and of the other witnesses, she died a second time in peace. And the devil fled in confusion.

[LM, Miracles II, 1; 3 Cel. 40]

27 - Confession of the Woman of Benevento

The miraculous episode recounted in this painting took place in the castle of Monte Marano, near Benevento. A woman, noble of both birth and virtue, was bound to Francis by great devotion. Since her illness had taken a turn for the worse, she was on her deathbed and she died around sunset. During her funeral wake, the people praying over her saw the women sit up in her bed and tell one of the priests who had been her spiritual director that she wanted to make her confession, because Francis had allowed her to return to her body so she could be pardoned for a serious sin that she had never confessed and that now barred her from eternal life. The woman and the priest, both trembling, performed the sacrament. Then, having been absolved, the women lay down calmly on the bed and died in peace. In the fresco, the devil is fleeing from the woman in disappointment and a providential angel replaces him in the action. In the upper left-hand corner, Francis is interceding with Christ.

BEATUS FRANCISCUS LIBERAVIT ISTUM CAPTIVUM ACCUSATUM DE HAERESI ET DE MANDATO DOMINI PAPAE RECOMMENDATUM SUB POENA EPISCOPA- TUS EPISCOPO TIBURTINO, ET HOC FUIT IN FESTO IPSIUS BEATI FRANCISCI CUIUS VIGILIAM IPSE CAPTIVUS DE MORE ECCLESIAE IEIUNAVERAT.

Blessed Francis freed this prisoner who had been accused of heresy under the orders of the Lord Pope and delivered to the Bishop of Tivoli, under the penalty of losing the epis- copate. And this came to pass on the vigil of this same Blessed Francis' feastday, when the prisoner had fasted as was the custom of the church.

[LM Miracles V, 4; 3 Cel. 93]

28 - Liberation of Pietro the heretic

The extensive cycle in the Upper Church in Assisi that illustrates the Legend of St. Francis is explicated in St. Bonaventure's account of the miracles that took place after Francis' death. According to this story, « when Gregory IX was pope, a man called Pietro from Alife was accused of heresy and taken prisoner at Rome, where the Pope gave him over to the bishop of Tivoli for safe-keeping. The bishop took him with his diocese as the forfeit, and put him in chains, throwing him into a dark dungeon from which there was no escape. There the prisoner was given a ration of food and drink. Then, hearing that it was the vigil of the feast of St. Francis, he entreated him with prayers and tears to have pity on him: he had now purified his faith and renounced all heresy and become a devout client of St. Francis who was one of Christ's most loyal servants. As a result, he was found worthy to be heard by God, through the merits of St. Francis. At twilight on the evening of his feastday, St. Francis took pity on him and came into his prison. He called him by name and told him to stand up. Pietro was terrified and asked who it was. He was told that it was St. Francis. There and then he saw the chains on his feet broken by the power of the Saint's presence. At the same time, some of the iron bolts fell from the stone walls of the cell, so that the walls opened and left the way free for him to escape. He was free but he was so overcome that he could not make his escape; instead he rushed to the door of the cell and frightened the guards with his cries. They told the bishop how he had been freed from his bonds and when he had heard the whole story, he visited the prison himself. There he realized clearly that the power of God had been at work and he fell down to worship him. The chains were shown to the pope and the cardinals and when they saw what had happened, they were amazed and gave thanks to God ». There are numerous differences in Tommaso of Celano's story, in which the episode takes place not in Alife of Catalonia but in the city of Alife located in southern Italy between the Volturno River and the Matese Mountains. However, the stories are identical in substance as far as the miracle itself is concerned. Francis, hovering on high, is interceding with God while the bishop, fully aware of the miracle, is kneeling before the prison as young Pietro leaves a free man. The people who had been attracted by his cries are now rejoicing in the power of the Lord. The vivid and fanciful architectural structures silhouetted against the empty background create a sort of mystical expectation. The massive red tower on the right is reminiscent of Trajan's column in Rome and the towering green structure on the left recalls the Septizonium built by Septimius Severus, an edifice that was also located in Rome but that was later destroyed.

Biographical notes on Giotto

The dates listed here make no pretence to accuracy, beginning with the very date of Giotto's birth, which according to Giorgio Vasari, was not in 1267 but 1276, or nine years later. On the other hand, it was Vasari who, perhaps due to a simple oversight, had also stated that there were thirty-two panels in the Upper Church, rather than twenty-eight. Thus, even in the most the reputable texts, the dates do vary, though not by much, and and are consequently still subject to debate.

1267 - Giotto, son of Bondone, is born in Vespignano in the Mugello Valley. Some say he was born in Florence.

From 1280 to 1290 - Giotto probably studied under Cenni di Pepi, known as "Cimabue" (1240-1302).

From 1290 to 1295 - Probable dates in which Giotto worked on the third and fourth bays of the Upper Church in Assisi (*Isaac blessing Jacob, Isaac rejecting Esau, Lamentation, Joseph is sold by his brothers, Joseph and his brothers in Egypt*). There are 36 frescoes in all, some of which are quite damaged. It also appears that Cimabue as well as the Roman School (Pietro Cavallini, Jacopo Torriti, Filippo Rusuti) also participated in their execution.

From 1296 to 1299 - Giotto paints the *Legend of St Francis*, totalling 28 frescoes, drawn from St. Bonaventure's *Major Life*. Giotto was commissioned to do this cycle by Brother Giovanni of Muro, who was Minister General of the Order of the Friars Minor at that time.

1300 - Giotto paints the loggia of the Lateran Basilica in Rome, commissioned by Boniface VIII, who proclaimed that year the first Jubilee Year of Christianity. The remnants of this fresco are now inside the Basilica of St. John Lateran, whereas a reproduction of the fresco in its entirety has been preserved in the Ambrosian Library in Milan (miniature in a manuscript by Jacopo Grimaldi, 1622).

From 1302 to 1306 - A culturally more mature Giotto frescoes the Arena Chapel in Padua (*Life of Joachim, Life of Mary, Life of Christ, The Last Judgement, Allegories of Virtues of Vices*) for a total of over one hundred representations, including the decorative motifs.

1310 - Giotto probably does the mosaic entitled *The Boat* in the portico of St. Peter's in Rome.

1314 - Giotto does the frescoes in the Magdalen Chapel in the Lower Church in Assisi. While the frescoes were probably conceived by Giotto, the actual painting was probably left mainly to his assistants.

1317 - Giotto does frescoes in the Palazzo della Ragione in Padua; the frescoes were lost in the fire of 1420.

From 1320 to 1325 - Giotto does frescoes in the Church of Santa Croce (Florence) -- in the Peruzzi Chapel (*Life of St John the Baptist and of St John the Evangelist*) and in the Bardi Chapel (*Life of St Francis*).

From 1328 to 1333 - Giotto is in Naples working for the Angevin king, Robert. All these works have been lost (Chapel in Castelnuovo, Castel dell'Ovo, Church of Santa Chiara, Church of the Incoronata).

1334 - Giotto is master builder for the works at the Duomo in Florence; he designs and builds the Bell Tower of Santa Maria del Fiore, which was later continued by Andrea Pisano, Francesco Talenti and others.

1337 - Giotto dies in Florence at the age of 70. The City of Florence has him buried in the Church of Santa Reparata with full honors.

1490 - Giotto's cenotaph is placed in the Duomo in Florence, with an epigraph by the poet Politian and a sculpture of the painter done by Benedetto da Maiano.

1901 - A monument, done by Italo Vagnetti, is erected in Vicchio in his honor.

Notes on the fundamental Franciscan biographies

Tommaso of Celano's First Life dates to 1229. It is usually referred to as the Legenda Gregorii, so named after Gregory IX, who approved it on February 2, 1229. Francis had died two years and four months before.

Tommaso of Celano's Second Life, also called Memoriale in desiderio animae, was written in 1246 following the request of Brother Crescentius of Jesi, who was elected Minister General in Genoa during the Chapter of 1244. He had also ordered each friar to relate anything he knew to be true about the founder of the Order.

Celano's two Lives are different in tone, but it is also true that it was precisely between 1230 and 1245 that the 'Spiritualists' (Observants, Zealots, Rigorists and Joachimists) were segregated from the Order. The Church of Rome had granted widespread exemptions in the lifestyle of the friars and to Francis' original followers, these new customs must have been equivalent to a betrayal. However, it was only by this means that the Order was able to grow, open schools and assume social commitments and ecclesiastical offices. Tommaso of Celano found himself in the midst of the fray and although he suffered because of the ideological controversy, he accepted the changes that had taken place. In his Second Life, he altered the description he had made in his First Life. But which version is closer to the truth? In her book, Il Francescanesimo di Fra' Tommaso da Celano, Silvana Spirito speaks of the « preeminence of the First Life over the Second Life as a way of understanding the Franciscan movement and all its contradictions. Nevertheless, the Second Life is always a highly interesting source, even though it is not the one that most adheres to the Saint's historical and spiritual reality. » As to the literary differences between the two Lives, Silvana Spirito says, « With regard to the style [of the Second Life], it is easy to note that, in comparison to the First Life, it is less forceful and solemn. It seems to us that a good part of the Second Life flows like a medieval Florilegia and does not have the distinctive character of a true historia. Furthermore, a lesser literary elaboration can be seen. Nevertheless, a shining simplicity and force of imagery alway predominate. »

After he had completed the Second Life, Thomas of Celano added the Treatise of Miracles (Tractatus de miraculis) between 1250 and 1253, following the request made by Brother Giovanni Buralli of Parma, General of the Order.

The General Chapter of Narbonne was held in 1260. The Minister General was the spiritualist Giovanni Buralli of Parma, whom the Pope had asked to resign to prevent the Order from being jeopardized by his Joachimist ideas. Then Bonaventure of Bagnoregio was elected and he was given the task of drawing up a new biography of the saint. St. Bonaventure was ready to present his work as early as 1263, during the Chapter of Pisa. The biography of St. Francis written by St. Bonaventure was later called the Legenda Maior or Major Life and not only was it the source used by Giotto for his frescoes in the Upper Church, but it was also Dante's inspiration for Cantos XI and XII of Paradiso in the Divine Comedy.

The so-called « Franciscan issue » is certainly not resolved in this work. Nevertheless, St. Bonaventure is said to be Francis' « conscience, » since he tried to impart a philosophical aspect to the Saint's emotions.

To complete the list of writings that are considered to be biographical works, even if unofficial ones, we have added the following, which can be found in the *St. Francis of Assisi, Writings and Early Biographies: English Omnibus of the Sources for the Life of St. Francis.*

Letter of Brother Elias, dated 1226; Letter of Greccio, dated 1246; *Legend of the Three Companions,* date uncertain; *Legend of Perugia*, dated to between the thirteenth and fourteenth century; *The Little Flowers of Francis of Assisi,* written between 1327 and 1340; *Sacrum Commercium*, probably dated to 1227; Canto XI of *Paradiso* by Dante Alighieri, written during the last years of Dante's life: he died in 1321.

A SELECT BIBLIOGRAPHY

BACCHESCHI and GIANCARLO VIGORELLI, *L'opera completa di Giotto*, Rizzoli, Milan, 1978.

BARGELLINI, PIERO, *I Fioretti di Santa Chiara,* Ed. Porziuncola, S. Maria degli Angeli, 1965.

BIGARONI, MARINO, *San Francesco d'Assisi - compilazione,* Ed. Porziuncola, S. Maria degli Angeli, 1975.

CARDINI, FRANCO, *Francesco d'Assisi*, Mondadori, Milan, 1989.

DANTE *Divine Comedy*, translated by Laurence Binyon. In *The Portable Dante*, ed. Paolo Milano, The Viking Press New York, 1947.

FABRETTI NAZZARENO et al. *Francesco e altro*, Mondadori, Milan 1982.

HABIG, M., ed. *St. Francis of Assisi, Writings and Early Biographies: English Omnibus of the Sources for the Life of St. Francis*, Franciscan Herald Press, Chicago 1972 [St. Bonaventure's *Legenda Maior,* Thomas of Celano's *First Life, Second Life and Treatise on the Miracles of Blessed Francis, Legend of the Three Companions, Legend of Perugia, Mirror of Perfection, Little Flowers of St. Francis*, and other thir- teenth-century testimonies].

JOERGENSEN, GIOVANNI, *San Francesco d'Assisi, Ed. Università, Perugia 1968.*

MAGRO, PASQUALE, *San Francesco d'Assisi,* Rome, 1981.

MAGRO, PASQUALE, « L'immagine di Francesco nella sua basilica di Assisi, » in *San Francesco*, Ed. Basilica di San Francesco, Assisi.

MARINANGELI, BONAVENTURA, « La serie di affreschi giotteschi rappresentanti la vita di San Francesco nella chiesa superiore di Assisi » in *Miscellanea francescana*, Foligno, 1911.

MILLOZZI, MICHEL, Various articles published in *San Francesco*, Ed. Francescana, Assisi, 1974.

THE NEW AMERICAN BIBLE, Thomas Nelson Publishers, Nashville, 1971.

RUF, GERHARD, *San Francesco e San Bonaventura*, Ed. Francescana, Assisi 1974.

SABATIER, PAUL, *Life of St. Francis of Assisi*, trans. Louise Seymour Houghton, Charles Scribner's Sons, New York, 1894.

SOLINAS, MARIO, *La Verna*, Ed. Grafica, Perugia, 1959.

SPIRITO, SILVANA, *Il Francescanesimo di Fra' Tommaso da Celano*, Ed. Porziuncola, S. Maria degli Angeli, 1963.

Abbreviations

1 Cel. = *First Life* by Thomas of Celano
2 Cel. = *Second Life* by Thomas of Celano
3 Cel. = *Treatise on the Miracles of Blessed Francis*
       by Thomas of Celano
LM = *Legenda Maior (Major Life)* by St. Bonaventure
LM, Miracles = *Legenda Maior. Miraculi* by St. Bonaventure
Leg. Per. = *Legend of Perugia*
LF = *Little Flowers of St. Francis*
Mirr. = *Mirror of Perfection*
Sab. = *Life of St. Francis of Assisi by Paul Sabatier*
Three Comp. = *Legend of the Three Companions*

INDEX OF NAMES AND PLACES

Printed by
Tipolitografia Porziuncola
Santa Maria degli Angeli – Assisi
March 1992